Say it First

Tools to Talk with Your Teen Before They're Targeted

by

Cerise Woodard

Watersprings
PUBLISHING

SAY IT FIRST by Cerise Woodard
Published by Watersprings Publishing,
P.O. Box 1284 Olive Branch, MS 38654
www.waterspringspublishing.com

Contact the publisher for bulk orders and permission requests.

Printed in the United States of America.

ISBN-13: 978-1-964972-22-0

For my daughter, the heartbeat of my passion. And for every child who deserves protection, and every caring adult who stands in the gap for them.

Say it First

Tools to Talk with Your Teen Before They're Targeted

Table of Contents

Foreword

When I began my work to protect children from exploitation—as a member of the United States Congress and later as the founder of Shared Hope International—I learned a difficult truth: while those who seek to exploit children continually adapt, many families are left without clear, practical guidance to keep their children safe. Today's digital world offers incredible opportunities for learning and connection, but it also creates space for subtle, patient forms of grooming and recruitment that often go unnoticed. This reality makes informed prevention more urgent than ever.

For decades, I have listened to survivors, families, law enforcement, and front line professionals, and one message remains consistent: prevention begins with informed, empowered adults who are willing to have honest conversations with the young people in their lives. Parents do not need to be experts to protect their children—but they do need tools, language, and confidence. This book provides exactly that. Grounded in clarity rather than fear, it offers practical, compassionate guidance rooted in relationships, communication, and trust.

I have seen both the consequences of missed warning signs and the power of early intervention. When caregivers understand grooming behaviors and respond with calm confidence, they become one of the strongest protective factors in a child's life. This book meets families where they are, offering realistic strategies for ongoing conversations that build awareness and resilience over time. Every child deserves a safe childhood, and every family deserves access to trustworthy information. My hope is that this resource sparks meaningful conversations and equips families to take lasting steps toward protecting our children.

Linda Smith,
Founder and President, Shared Hope International

Introduction

Before You Begin — Note to Parents

Being a parent in today's world is both a gift and a challenge. We want to protect our kids, but the dangers they face—online, in relationships, and even among peers—aren't always obvious. It can feel overwhelming to know where to start or how to have the kind of conversations that really matter.

That's why this book was written.

It's not meant to scare you—it's meant to equip you. Each chapter focuses on a theme that teens today are navigating, from manipulation and consent to online safety and building self-worth. You'll find real stories, conversation prompts, and quick reference "cheat sheets" to help you bring these topics into everyday conversations.

Here's how to use this book:

- **Go at your own pace.** You don't have to read cover to cover. Choose the chapters that feel most urgent, or work through one each week.

- **Use the prompts.** They're designed to spark honest discussion, not lectures.

- **Come back often.** These aren't one-time talks—they're ongoing conversations.

The goal isn't perfection—it's connection. If you keep the door open, your teen will know where to turn when it matters most.

Too many kids fall for the trap, not because they're reckless—but because no one told them what to look out for.

#sayitfirst

Chapter 1:
Silence Isn't Safety

Something has shifted—and it's more dangerous than most of us want to admit.

Right now, teens are being targeted, manipulated, and exploited at alarming rates. The rise in online predators, sextortion, intimate partner violence, and grooming tactics has created a silent epidemic. Every scroll, every click, every message opens a door—and too often, no one is standing guard.

What's worse? These dangers don't always look like danger.

Sometimes, it looks like a new friend.

A cute stranger who seems to really understand.

A controlling boyfriend masked as someone "who just cares a lot."

A group chat that turns into pressure.

A DM that starts off fun—and ends in threats.

Too many kids fall for the trap, not because they're reckless—but because no one told them what to look out for. And too many parents stay silent, not because they don't care—but because they don't know how to start the conversation without fear, shame, or shutting their child down.

That's why this book exists.

As a forensic nurse and advocate who has sat with victims, heard the pain, and seen the aftermath, I know firsthand: most of these tragedies are preventable. Not by scaring kids into silence, but by talking to them early, openly, and often. Silence is no longer safe. And hope is not a strategy. Over the years, I've had the privilege of speaking with schools, faith leaders, community organizations, and healthcare professionals about these very issues. Each conversation reinforces what I know to be true: when parents and caring adults are equipped to talk openly with young people, we can close the gaps predators exploit.

This is not a book filled with lectures. It's not a rulebook either. It's a guide for conversations—real ones. Honest ones. The kind that builds trust. The kind that helps your teen spot the difference between love and control, safety and danger, privacy and secrecy. The kind that gives your teen the tools to think critically and speak up, before someone else teaches them the hard way.

No parent wants to believe it could happen to their child. But the truth is, this kind of optimistic bias may leave your child unprepared when approached by an offender.

Silence is no longer safe.

This book will help you say what needs to be said—before someone else does.

The Urgent Reality: Online Enticement Is Rising

The dangers facing teens today are not just hypothetical—they are real, rapidly evolving, and affecting children younger than ever before.

According to the National Center for Missing & Exploited Children (NCMEC):

- From 2020 to 2023, 476 children were reported missing due to online enticement.

- 59% of those children were 15 years old or younger, and nearly 1 in 5 (18%) were just 13 or younger.

- A staggering 92% were known to be speaking with adults online before their disappearance.

- 20% had already met an offender in person after first engaging with them online.

- Over one-third (36%) were recovered in a different state, showing just how far a child might travel under manipulation—often with travel funded by the offender through rideshare apps, tickets, or money-sending apps.

- Offenders were overwhelmingly male and often significantly older than the victim—41% were more than 10 years older, with a median age gap of 10 years.

- The most common platforms used to lure children included Snapchat, TikTok, Discord, Instagram, and Facebook. Some children were approached on multiple platforms simultaneously.

This is not just "stranger danger." These are targeted manipulations, often slow and calculated—built on trust, secrecy, and emotional connection.

Parents can no longer afford to assume "my kid would never…" Predators are counting on your silence and your child's curiosity.

This is why this book matters. It's not just about protection—it's about preparation. It's about having conversations that can close the gaps before someone else exploits them.

The Hidden Epidemic: Teen Dating Violence

Healthy boundaries aren't just nice to have—they're essential. Why? Because teen dating violence (TDV) is alarmingly common—and often hidden in plain sight. (https://www.thehotline.org/stakeholders/domestic-violence-statistics/)

According to the Centers for Disease Control's (CDC) 2021 Youth Risk Behavior Survey https://www.cdc.gov/intimate-partner-violence/about/about-teen-dating-violence.html:

- About 1 in 12 high school students experienced physical dating violence in the past year.

- Nearly 1 in 10 experienced sexual dating violence during that same period.

Broader studies show even greater numbers:

- Up to 1.5 million high school students experience physical abuse from a dating partner annually-Centers for Disease Control and Prevention, "Physical Dating Violence Among High School Students—United States, 2003," Morbidity and Mortality Weekly Report, May 19, 2006, Vol. 55, No. 19.

- Roughly 1 in 3 adolescents—that's ~33%—experience physical, sexual, emotional, or verbal abuse in a dating relationship. Davis, Antoinette, MPH. 2008. Interpersonal and Physical Dating Violence among Teens. The National Council on Crime and Delinquency Focus.
  But it gets more alarming:

- Only 33% of abused teens ever tell anyone - Liz Claiborne Inc., conducted by Teenage Research Unlimited, (February 2005)—and 50% of youth who experience both dating violence and rape attempt suicide D. M. Ackard, Minneapolis, MN, and D. Neumark-Sztainer, Division of Epidemiology, School of Public Health, University of Minnesota, Minneapolis, MN, Date Violence and Date Rape Among Adolescents: Associations with Disordered Eating Behaviors and Psychological Health, Child Abuse & Neglect, 26 455-473, (2002).

- And teen victims are much more likely to face depression, anxiety, substance abuse, and ongoing intimate partner violence into adulthood.

Why These Stats Matter

- **It's not rare—it's widespread.** One of the most cited statistics is that "1 in 3 teens" will experience physical, emotional, or sexual abuse in a relationship. It's real—and likely underreported.

- **It's not only physical:** Emotional, verbal, and online abuses are equally destructive and often harder to spot.

- **It's not harmless:** The ripple effects are serious and lasting—mental health issues, risky behaviors, future abuse.

- **It's not obvious:** Most teens keep it a secret and don't ask for help, meaning parents may have no clue.

That's why early, open conversations about healthy relationships and boundaries are vital. This isn't just a teen chapter topic—it's a foundational piece of this guide.

Kids can't defend themselves from what they don't understand.

#sayitfirst

Chapter 2:
What is Manipulation, Really?

Names and identifying details have been changed. This story is based on a real experience shared during advocacy work. It has been edited for clarity and presented in a way that's relatable and age-appropriate for teens and parents alike.

Ashley met him at her after-school job. He was older, charming, and had a car—which made him feel more mature than the boys her age.

After a few casual conversations, he asked for her number. Their first date felt exciting and grown-up. She didn't know it yet, but this was the beginning of a pattern she would come to recognize as manipulation.

At first, he was sweet and attentive. He texted good morning, made her laugh, and gave her cute nicknames. He told her things like, "You're not like other girls" and "I've never felt this way before."

Even after a night when he ignored her boundaries and crossed a serious line (you'll hear more about that later), she stayed—because part of her still wanted to believe in the good parts of him.

Looking back, she realized the charm was a mask. It covered the part of him that didn't respect her "no." It wasn't love—it was control disguised as care.

UNDERSTANDING GROOMING, EMOTIONAL PRESSURE, AND WHY "TRUST" CAN BE DANGEROUS WHEN MISUSED IS CRITICALLY IMPORTANT

Most parents think they'll know when someone is manipulating their child. They picture a creepy stranger in a van or someone saying inappropriate things right away.

But that's not how it usually happens.

Manipulation is slow, strategic, and disguised as something good. And that's exactly what makes it dangerous.

What Is Manipulation?

Manipulation is when someone tries to influence or control another person's thoughts, feelings, or actions—without their full awareness or consent.

It often comes across as:

- Flattery or praise that feels too good to be true
- Guilt-tripping ("If you cared about me, you'd…")
- Withholding affection or giving silent treatment
- Threats, ultimatums, or using secrets as leverage
- Making someone feel responsible for *their* emotions or actions

The goal? To slowly break down boundaries and gain control—without the person even realizing it's happening.

What Is Grooming?

Grooming is a type of manipulation specifically used by

predators—especially when targeting minors.

Grooming is a step-by-step process where the predator builds trust, creates emotional attachment, and isolates the child to gain access, influence, or even physical control.

Here's what that can look like:

Stages of Grooming

1. **Targeting a Vulnerability**

   Predators look for kids who seem lonely, insecure, isolated, or emotionally unsupervised. Social media makes this easy.

2. **Gaining Trust**

   They become the "cool older friend," the "only one who gets you," or the one who always listens. It feels comforting—but it's calculated.

3. **Filling a Need**

   They give gifts, attention, advice, compliments, or validation—often things the child feels they're not getting at home or school.

4. **Isolation**

   Slowly, they turn the teen away from others: "Your parents just don't get it," or "Don't tell your friends— they'll ruin it." This creates secrecy and dependence.

5. **Sexualization or Control**

   The conversation turns inappropriate, or the pressure ramps up. The predator may ask for pictures, meet-ups, or make emotional threats.

6. **Keeping Them Silent**

   They may use shame, fear, or guilt to keep the child

quiet: "You'll get in trouble too," or "No one will believe you."

Manipulation Isn't Always Obvious

It's important to help teens understand that **manipulators often seem kind, charming, and trustworthy—at first**. They play a role. They mirror your child's personality. They make the interaction feel *special*—not scary.

That's why so many teens say later, *"I didn't know what was happening"* or *"It didn't feel wrong at first."*

Predator Patterns: What Parents Should Watch For

- Older individuals developing overly close relationships with your child

- Excessive private communication (texts, DMs, video chats)

- Giving gifts, money, or attention

- Suggesting they keep secrets

- Emotional highs and lows (love-bombing, guilt, withdrawal)

- Encouraging emotional dependence or "us against the world" thinking

Conversation Starters for Parents

Here are a few ways to introduce the topic in a nonthreatening way:

- *"What would you do if a friend asked you to keep a secret that made you feel uncomfortable?"*

- *"What's the strangest thing a friend ever asked you to do?"*

- *"Have you ever seen someone acting super different online than in real life?"*

- *"Has anyone ever given you a weird vibe, like they weren't who they said they were?"*

- *"If you could build your perfect friend from scratch, what qualities would they have?"*

- *"Have you ever heard the word grooming used online? What do you think it means?"*

- *"Who's the most trustworthy person you know, and what makes them that way?"*

- *"Have you ever had a friend who started hanging out with a new crowd and changed a lot?"*

- *"Sometimes people act really nice just to get something. What do you think that looks like?"*

Final Thought: *Give Them Language Before They Need It*

Kids can't defend themselves from what they don't understand. When you help your teen **recognize manipulation and grooming**, you give them the power to name what's happening—and walk away.

This chapter isn't about fear. It's about **awareness**.

When teens can say, *"That doesn't feel right,"*—you've already won half the battle.

- "If someone you trusted made you feel guilty for saying no—how would you handle that?"

- "Do you think it's still manipulation if someone doesn't *force* you—but pressures you emotionally?"

Parent Power Points: What is Manipulation, Really?

Recognizing Manipulation & Grooming

Red Flags of Manipulation

- Guilt-tripping: "If you loved me, you'd…"

- Love-bombing: Over-the-top affection or attention too quickly

- Isolation: Turning your teen against friends or family

- Secret-keeping: "Don't tell anyone about this"

- Emotional dependence: "You're the only one who gets me"

- Flattery that seems excessive or too personal

- Using jealousy, shame, or fear to gain control

Stages of Grooming to Watch For

- Targeting: Scanning for emotionally vulnerable teens (especially online)

- Trust-building: Frequent messaging, compliments, shared 'secrets'

- Filling a need: Gifts, attention, support

- Isolation: Discouraging other relationships, emphasizing secrecy

- Sexualization or control: Requests for explicit images or meet-ups

- Silencing: Using guilt, fear, or threats to keep the child quiet

Quick Tips for Parents

- Stay curious, not controlling—ask, don't interrogate.

- Normalize conversations about red flags and online interactions.

- Reassure your teen they can come to you—even if they've made a mistake.

- Use examples from movies, shows, or social media to spark dialogue.

- Watch for sudden changes in mood, secrecy, or online habits.

Your job isn't to choose who they love—but to equip them to choose wisely.
#sayitfirst

Chapter 3:
Real Love vs. Toxic Attachment

After their rocky beginning, Ashley tried to focus on the version of him that made her feel special.

But that version didn't last.

He started getting jealous when she spent time with friends. If she didn't answer his texts fast enough, he'd blow up her phone with angry messages. When she tried to pull away, he'd beg or cry or make promises to change.

Then he'd flip back to sweet—showing up with flowers, apologizing, telling her they were soulmates. That no one would ever love her like he did.

It was confusing and exhausting. But also… intoxicating.

Ashley felt like maybe this was love, just the complicated kind. She didn't know how to explain it to anyone. And honestly, part of her thought if she could just love him hard enough, he'd stop crossing lines.

It took time—and distance—for her to see what was really going on: a pattern of emotional manipulation and toxic attachment that left her questioning herself more than him.

HELPING YOUR TEEN RECOGNIZE THE DIFFERENCE BETWEEN CARE AND CONTROL

We all want our kids to experience real love—kind, respectful, and supportive relationships that make them feel seen and safe. But too often, what teens *think* is love is actually control in disguise.

In a world where toxic relationships are romanticized in songs, shows, and social media, it's crucial to help teens tell the difference between real connection and emotional dependency.

What Healthy Love Looks Like

A healthy relationship is built on:

- Mutual respect
- Trust without constant surveillance
- Open communication
- Support for each other's growth
- Freedom to set boundaries without fear

In a healthy relationship, your teen feels:

- ✓ Safe
- ✓ Heard
- ✓ Respected
- ✓ Empowered to say "no" without guilt
- ✓ Able to be themselves without pressure

What Toxic Attachment Feels Like

Toxic attachment might feel exciting or intense at first, but it often includes:

- Constant check-ins that become controlling
- Jealousy disguised as love: "I just don't want anyone else looking at you"
- Love-bombing followed by emotional withdrawal

- Possessiveness or keeping your teen away from others
- Mood swings that keep your teen walking on eggshells

Over time, it becomes less about connection and more about control.

Common Misbeliefs Teens May Have

- *"Jealousy just means they care."*
- *"We fight because we're passionate."*
- *"They just need me. I can help them."*
- *"It's normal to always be texting—if not, they'll get mad."*

These aren't signs of love—they're red flags.

Warning Signs of Abuse Disguised as Love

Teach your teen to look out for behaviors like:

- Monitoring their phone or social media
- Getting angry if they talk to others
- Controlling what they wear, who they hang out with, or how they act
- Apologizing with gifts or guilt instead of changed behavior
- Blaming *them* for the other person's anger or bad behavior

Conversation Starters for Parents

Start these when you're driving, watching a show, or scrolling TikTok together:

- *"Do you think jealousy means love? Why or why not?"*

- *"What do you think a respectful relationship feels like?"*

- *"If someone gets mad when you set a boundary, is that love?"*

- *"What would you say to a friend who was dating someone super possessive?"*

- *"What do you think makes a relationship healthy vs. toxic?"*

- *"Has anyone ever made you feel uncomfortable, even if they didn't do anything obvious?"*

- *"If a stranger started talking to you and seemed super nice, how would you react?"*

- *"Do you think it's possible to be too nice to someone? Why or why not?"*

- *"Have you ever had a gut feeling that something wasn't right? What did you do?"*

- *"If someone made a joke that made you feel weird, what would you do?"*

- *"What would you do if someone older than you gave you too many compliments?"*

- *"How do you set boundaries when someone doesn't seem to take the hint?"*

- *"What's your plan if you ever need to get out of a situation fast?"*

- *"What's the best excuse to leave a situation that feels off?"*

Final Thought: *Don't Wait for Them to Experience It*

Real love builds you up. Toxic attachment tears you down. And too many teens don't realize the difference until they're deep in it.

Your job isn't to choose who they love—but to equip them to choose wisely. By helping them spot the signs early, you give them the tools to walk away from toxic patterns before they take root.

Parent Power Points: Real Love vs. Toxic Attachment

Real Love vs. Toxic Attachment

Signs of Healthy Love

- Respects your teen's boundaries and decisions
- Encourages their independence and friendships
- Listens without judgment
- Supports their goals and dreams
- Accepts "no" without guilt or punishment
- Communicates openly and honestly

Red Flags of Toxic Attachment

- Gets jealous easily or accuses them of cheating
- Checks their phone or social media without permission
- Demands constant contact or quick replies
- Isolates them from friends or family
- Uses guilt, threats, or gifts to control behavior
- Has intense highs and lows in the relationship

Conversation Starters

- *"What do you think a healthy relationship looks like?"*

- *"How do you think people show love in respectful ways?"*

- *"What would you do if someone you cared about started controlling you?"*

- *"Do you think jealousy is ever a good thing in a relationship?"*

- *"Have you seen toxic relationships in shows or on social media? What stood out to you?"*

> **Let's be honest, most parents are more comfortable talking about curfews and chores than they are about consent.**

#sayitfirst

Chapter 4:
Talk About Consent Like You Talk About Curfews

Ashley was 17 when she met an older guy while working a part-time job after school. He was charming, had a car, and made her feel grown. Their first date was fun—he made her laugh, listened to her, and treated her like she mattered.

Later that night, they ended up back at his place. While hanging out in his room, they started kissing. But when things started going further, Ashley felt uncomfortable. She told him "No." He didn't listen.

Instead, he said, "You know you want this." She said, "No" again. But he kept pushing—insisting, grabbing, holding her down. "It'll only be a minute," he whispered.

So she gave up. Not because she wanted to. But because it didn't seem like she had another choice.

Afterward, he apologized and said, "I just couldn't help myself—you're so sexy." Ashley didn't know what to think. Was that a compliment? Was it her fault? No one had ever talked to her about situations like this. So, she stayed quiet.

HOW TO NORMALIZE CONVERSATIONS ABOUT BOUNDARIES, AUTONOMY, AND RESPECT

Let's be honest—most parents are more comfortable talking about curfews and chores than they are about consent.

But if your teen is old enough to have a phone, stay out late, or date... they're old enough to know what **bodily autonomy** and **mutual respect** mean.

And they're definitely old enough to know that real consent isn't just about saying "no"—it's about learning how to say "yes" in a safe, healthy, and pressure-free environment.

What Is Consent, Really?

Consent is **freely given, enthusiastic, informed, ongoing, and reversible.**

Here's what that means:

- **Freely given:** It's not pressured, manipulated, or coerced.

- **Enthusiastic:** It's a genuine yes, not a tired or scared "fine."

- **Informed:** Everyone knows what they're agreeing to.

- **Ongoing:** Just because someone said yes once doesn't mean always.

- **Reversible:** Consent can be taken back at any time, for any reason.

Consent Is More Than "No Means No"

Many teens don't fully understand that:

- Silence is not consent.

- Freezing or laughing nervously doesn't mean "yes."

- A "yes" under pressure is not real consent.
- Consent under the influence (alcohol, drugs) is not valid.

It's also important they know:

- Consent isn't just for sex. It applies to hugging, touching, kissing, sharing images, and even flirting.
- You don't owe anyone access to your body—not even if you're dating.

Coercion vs. Consent: The Gray Area No One Talks About

Coercion is when someone uses **guilt, pressure, or threats** to get what they want. It sounds like:

- "You said you liked me. Why won't you prove it?"
- "We've done it before—what's the big deal?"
- "If you don't send a pic, I'll find someone who will."

That's not consent. That's control.

Helping your teen recognize coercion in the moment is one of the best protections you can give them.

The Porn Problem

Many teens (and even adults) form their first ideas about sex from porn—and that's a problem. Porn often shows aggression, nonverbal or ignored boundaries, and unrealistic power dynamics. If teens are learning about relationships from porn, they may:

- Think it's normal not to ask for consent
- Believe "rough" behavior is expected
- Confuse dominance with love or attraction
- Fail to recognize their own discomfort

It's important to say: **"That's not real. That's not healthy. That's not how you learn about respect or connection."**

 # Conversation Starters for Parents

Open up conversations in simple, honest ways:

- *"What's your definition of 'too close for comfort'?" "How do you decide if a hug or touch from someone is okay?"*

- *"Let's come up with a 'safe word' or phrase you could use in case you ever need help without explaining?"*

- *"What does consent mean to you? Do you think people really understand it?"*

- *"Have you ever seen something on a show or online that didn't look like real consent?" "What would you do if someone pressured you after you already said no?"*

- *"Do you feel like people your age talk about boundaries or just avoid them?" "Can you imagine how you'd respond if a friend told you someone crossed a line?"*

- *"Has anyone ever made you feel uncomfortable, even if they didn't do anything obvious?"*

- *"How do you set boundaries when someone doesn't seem to take the hint?"*

- *"What would you do if someone older than you gave you too many compliments?"*

A Note on Porn Addiction

Some teens aren't just exposed to porn—they're **consuming it regularly**. What might have started as curiosity can escalate into compulsive behavior, shaping how they see intimacy, relationships, and themselves.

Porn addiction in teens can lead to:

- Desensitization to real-world affection

- Escalation into more aggressive or extreme content

- Shame, secrecy, and isolation

- Struggles with self-esteem, impulse control, or emotional regulation

If your child or teen seems withdrawn, preoccupied, or defensive around the topic of porn—or if they tell you they're struggling—**approach with compassion, not punishment.** Shame only deepens the silence.

Instead, connect them with resources that offer education and support.

Helpful resource: https://www.fightthenewdrug.org This site offers teen-friendly, science-based, and non-religious content that helps young people understand the impact of porn and find healthier ways forward.

Parent Power Points: Talking About Consent

Key Points About Consent

- Consent must be freely given, informed, enthusiastic, ongoing, and reversible.

- Silence or passive behavior is not consent.

- Consent can be withdrawn at any time—even in the middle of an activity.

- Being under the influence of drugs or alcohol means someone cannot legally consent.

- Consent isn't just about sex—it applies to all forms of physical interaction and digital boundaries.

Signs of Coercion or Gray Areas

- Using guilt or pressure: "If you really loved me…"

- Bringing up past behavior to justify current pressure: "We've already done this before."

- Threatening to leave or find someone else if your teen doesn't comply.

- Implying they're 'boring' or 'immature' for saying no.

- Making someone feel unsafe or obligated for setting a boundary, so that saying "no" no longer feels like an option.

Conversation Starters

- *"What do you think consent means in a relationship?"*

- *"Have you ever seen a situation on a show or online where someone ignored boundaries?"*

- *"How would you support a friend who felt pressured to do something they weren't ready for?"*

- *"Do people at your school talk about what healthy consent looks like?"*

- *"What would you want a partner to do if you said no?"*

Resource for Porn Addiction Support

If your teen is struggling with compulsive porn use or exposure, visit https://www.fightthenewdrug.org — a teen-friendly, non-religious, science-based resource for understanding porn's impact and finding help.

For most teens, the screen isn't optional—it's where they socialize, express themselves, and explore identity.

#sayitfirst

Chapter 5:
When Screens Become Traps

This is a composite story inspired by real scenarios shared in advocacy and prevention work. Names and identifying details have been changed to protect privacy

Malik was 14 when he got a DM from someone named "Bri." She had a cute profile picture, said she was 15, and claimed she went to a nearby school. Bri was friendly, funny, and seemed to really get him. They started messaging every day—at first about school and music, but soon it became more personal.

Bri complimented Malik's photos, asked questions about his life, and told him she thought he was cute. Malik hadn't really dated before, so it felt good to be noticed. They shared jokes, playlists, and inside comments. Eventually, Bri started calling him her boyfriend.

Then one night, she asked for a photo. "Just something private, just for me," she said. When Malik hesitated, she replied, "Come on, don't you trust me? We're basically together." He didn't want to lose the connection—so he sent it. Then came another request. Then another.

And then, silence. Bri stopped responding.

A few days later, a new message came from a different account. This person claimed they had all of Malik's photos— and if he didn't send more, they'd be shared online. Panicked and scared, Malik finally told his older cousin, who helped him talk to his mom.

They reported it to the authorities. The investigation revealed that "Bri" wasn't a girl at all. It was a 32-year-old man who had created fake profiles to lure in young boys. Malik felt ashamed—but also relieved. It took courage to speak up. That conversation was the start of healing, learning, and new boundaries around online safety.

HELPING YOUR TEEN STAY SAFE IN A WORLD WHERE CONNECTION CAN TURN TO EXPLOITATION FAST

We live in a digital world. For most teens, the screen isn't optional—it's where they socialize, express themselves, and explore identity. But behind those screens are risks many families don't talk about until it's too late.

Online predators no longer need to lurk in the shadows—they can just DM your child.

Digital Vulnerability: More Than Stranger Danger

Predators don't show up at the door anymore—they show up in the apps your teen uses every day:

- **Snapchat**
- **Instagram**
- **TikTok**
- **Discord**
- **Gaming platforms with chat functions**

And they don't start with threats. They start with kindness. Likes. Compliments. Common interests. They act like they "get it"—until they get what they want.

What Is Sextortion?

Sextortion is a form of blackmail. A predator convinces a teen to share a sexual image or video, and then uses it to:

- Demand more images or videos
- Threaten to release it to friends, family, or social media
- Force silence through fear and shame
- Demand money or to meet in person

Here's what parents MUST know:

- Boys are increasingly being targeted, especially in financial sextortion schemes.
- The predator may pretend to be a peer or use fake profiles to build trust.
- Many victims never tell anyone due to deep shame, fear, or guilt.
- Sadly, some teens have died by suicide because of sextortion pressure.

This is not just about bad decisions—it's about targeted manipulation by offenders who know exactly what they're doing.

DM (Direct Message) Culture & Risky Apps

Many teens treat DMs like private worlds. But predators thrive on secrecy. Risks increase when:

- Your teen uses anonymous chat apps or sites (e.g., Omegle, Whisper)

- They hide second accounts ("finstas" or "vault apps")

- There are no privacy settings or boundaries about who can message them

- They feel like they "can handle it" and don't need adult input

The Role of Secrecy & Shame

Predators use these tools like weapons:

- **Shame:** "You should be embarrassed. No one will understand."

- **Threats:** "I'll send this to your family if you don't do what I say."

- **Guilt:** "This is your fault. You're in too deep now."

This is why digital safety isn't just about filters or monitoring—it's about relationships, trust, and honest conversations before anything happens.

What Parents Can Do

- Talk early and often about what is and isn't okay online

- Teach teens they can always come to you—even if they made a mistake

- Discuss the risks without shaming them

- Set clear digital boundaries but focus on empowerment, not fear

Conversation Starters for Parents

- *"What's the funniest thing you ever posted online?"*

- *"Do you make friends with random people online?"*

- *"If someone famous randomly DM'ed you, what would you do?"*

- *"Have you ever gotten a weird or creepy message from someone you don't know?"*

- *"What's the best way to tell if someone online is actually who they say they are?"*

- *"If a stranger offered you money or gifts online, what would you think?"*

- *"Have you ever seen someone get pressured to do something on social media?"*

- *"What do you think about people who share their location online?"*

- *"What's the strangest follow request you've ever gotten?"*

- *"If someone asked for a picture of you, but it felt weird, what would you do?"*

- *"What would you do if a friend were talking to someone online that seemed sketchy?"*

- *"What would you do if someone asked you for a photo you weren't comfortable sending?"*

- *"What if someone DM'ed you saying they know exactly how you feel in response to your post?"*

- *"Have you ever heard of someone getting blackmailed online?"*

- *"Do you think it's easy to tell who's real or fake online?"*

- *"What apps do your friends use that feel risky to you?"*

- *"What would help you feel safe telling me if something went wrong online?"*

- *"What's your plan if you ever need to get out of a situation fast?"*

Final Thought: *Secrecy Is the Real Trap*

You can't prevent every message, app, or risk. But you can create a home where your teen knows they won't be punished for telling the truth.

Shame keeps teens silent. Fear keeps them trapped. Openness, connection, and proactive conversations are the way out.

Parent Power Points: Online Safety & Sextortion Awareness

Key Digital Dangers to Watch For

- Strangers initiating contact on social media or gaming platforms

- Teens hiding secondary accounts or using anonymous chat apps

- Requests for photos or videos that escalate to threats (sextortion)

- Use of shame, guilt, or threats to force silence

- Fake profiles pretending to be peers or influencers

What Is Sextortion?

- Predators manipulate teens into sending explicit images, then blackmail them.

- Boys are increasingly targeted in financial sextortion schemes.

- Victims often stay silent due to shame, fear, or guilt.

- Some teens have taken their lives due to sextortion-related trauma.

- It's not about bad choices—it's about targeted exploitation.

Conversation Starters

- *"Do you know what sextortion is? What would you do if someone threatened you online?"*

- *"Can you tell when someone is pretending to be a teen online?"*

- *"What would help you feel safe coming to me if something like this happened?"*

- *"Have you seen risky behavior or accounts online that make you uncomfortable?"*

- *"What should someone do if they made a mistake online and are scared to tell?"*

Resource for Teens in Crisis

- Visit https://www.missingkids.org/. "NCMEC is the nation's largest and most influential child protection organization. We lead the fight to protect children, creating vital resources for them and the people who keep them safe."

- Visit https://report.cybertip.org/. The Cyber Tipline is the place to report child sexual exploitation.

- Visit https://takeitdown.ncmec.org/. "Take It Down is a free service that can help you remove or stop the online sharing of nude, partially nude, or sexually explicit images or videos taken of you when you were under 18 years old. You can remain anonymous while using the service, and you won't have to send your images or videos to anyone."

- Visit https://www.missingkids.org/netsmartz. "NetSmartz is NCMEC's online safety education program. It provides age-appropriate videos and activities to help teach children to be safer online and more aware of potential online risks, and empower them to help prevent victimization by making safer choices on- and offline."

- Visit https://www.missingkids.org/education/kidsmartz. "KidSmartz is a child safety program that educates families about preventing abduction and empowers kids in grades K-5 to practice safer behaviors. This program offers resources to help parents, caregivers, and teachers protect kids by teaching and practicing the 4 Rules of Personal Safety using classroom lessons, at-home lessons, parent tips, and fun printable activities."

"

Whether it's a friend, a romantic interest, a YouTuber, or someone in their DMs—someone is always in their ear.

"

#sayitfirst

Chapter 6:
Who's in Their Ear?

This is a composite story inspired by real scenarios shared in advocacy and prevention work. Names and identifying details have been changed to protect privacy

Jalen was 15 when he started dating Mariah. She was smart, beautiful, and popular—everyone thought they made a great couple. His friends would tease him and hype him up. "You two are goals," they'd say. He liked her, but something about the relationship always felt a little… off.

Mariah had a way of twisting things. If he didn't text back fast enough, she'd say he didn't care. If he didn't post her on his stories, she'd accuse him of hiding her. She'd get upset when he hung out with friends—even his longtime best friend, who was a girl.

Whenever he tried to take a step back, she would cry or guilt him: "I've told you everything. If you leave me now, I'll fall apart." Jalen didn't want to hurt her. And he didn't want to be the bad guy. So, he stayed.

One day after practice, his coach pulled him aside. "You haven't been yourself lately," he said. "Something going on?" Jalen opened up a little—not everything, just enough to say he felt drained. His coach didn't push. He just said, "You don't have to stay in anything that's breaking you down."

That stuck with him. It took a few more weeks, but eventually Jalen ended the relationship. It was hard, but he started to feel like himself again. He learned that pressure can come in all forms—not just from peers, but even from someone who says they love you. And real love should never feel like pressure.

HELPING TEENS RECOGNIZE THE INFLUENCE BEHIND THE VOICES THEY FOLLOW

Teens are rarely making decisions in a vacuum. Whether it's a friend, romantic interest, a YouTuber, or someone in their DMs—someone is always in their ear.

That "someone" might encourage confidence and growth… Or they might normalize toxic behavior, push risky choices, or undermine everything you've taught them.

What Influence Looks Like in 2026

Today, influence isn't just about peer pressure in the school hallway. It's digital. Constant. Sometimes invisible.

Your teen is exposed to:

- **Influencers and content creators** pushing ideas about beauty, relationships, money, or sex
- **Older friends or romantic partners** who blur boundaries
- **Group chats or friend circles** where toxic behavior is normalized
- **Celebrities or "mentors"** who claim to offer empowerment—but actually exploit attention

And because teens are figuring out who they are, these voices often carry more weight than yours. That doesn't mean they don't respect you—it just means they're developing their own identity.

Your job? **Teach them how to think critically**—not just who to listen to.

Trust Isn't Always a Green Flag

Teens often say, "But I trust them."

That doesn't mean the influence is healthy.

- You can trust someone who pressures you.
- You can trust someone who isolates you.
- You can trust someone who sounds smart but is leading you into danger.

Trust should be earned over time, backed by respect, safety, and consistent behavior. It's not enough to feel understood—it has to be healthy.

How to Help Your Teen Self-Check

Help your teen build a mental filter. Encourage questions like:

- "Do I feel pressure to impress this person?"
- "Can I say no to them and still feel safe?"
- "Do they make me feel small, stupid, or unsure about myself?"
- "Would I act the same if my parents or safe adults were watching?"

If the answer to any of these is yes—it's a sign they may be under an **unhealthy influence**.

Influence by Adults or Older Teens

Not all adult attention is good attention.
Not every "mentor" is safe.
Not every older romantic partner is respectful.

Older individuals who show too much interest in a teen's personal life, isolate them, or push them into grown-up conversations too soon are crossing a line—whether or not they break a law.

Teach your teen that flattery doesn't equal safety. And age gaps don't equal maturity.

What Parents Can Do

- Be curious, not controlling: "Who do you like watching or listening to?"

- Watch or listen with them sometimes. Discuss, don't dismiss.

- Model healthy discernment: "I used to follow this person until I realized their message wasn't for me."

- Help them explore their values so they can identify when something *feels off.*

- Stay connected—*your voice is still their anchor*, even if it's quieter.

Conversation Starters for Parents

- *"What makes someone worth listening to?"*

- *"Who's your go-to person for advice when things feel confusing?"*

- *"If something bad happened, what's the first thing you'd want me to do to help?"*

- *"What's the one thing I can do to make sure you always feel safe talking to me?"*

- *"How do you know when you can trust an adult?"*

- *"What's the best way for parents to help without being annoying?"*

- *"What's one safety tip you think every teen should know?"*

- *"If you ever felt stuck in a situation you didn't like, what's the first thing you'd do?"*

- *"Have you ever followed someone online, then realized later they were problematic?"*

- *"Do your friends ever pressure you in ways that don't feel like pressure at first?"*

- *"What kind of advice would you trust from someone older than you?"*

Final Thought:
Influence Isn't Always Obvious

Sometimes the most dangerous voices are the ones that whisper instead of shout.

By helping your teen recognize influence, name it, and challenge it, you give them one of the most powerful tools they'll ever have: **discernment**.

Parent Power Points: Who's in Their Ear?

Identifying Influence & Discernment

Signs of Unhealthy Influence

- Makes your teen feel guilty for saying no
- Discourages them from listening to parents or other trusted adults
- Pushes them toward risky behaviors or secretive communication
- Triggers self-doubt, shame, or confusion
- Demands loyalty or isolates them from friends/family

Traits of Healthy Influence

- Encourages self-worth and independence
- Supports boundaries and respects 'no'
- Builds your teen up without manipulation or pressure
- Challenges them in healthy ways without belittling
- Helps them feel safe when being honest or imperfect

Conversation Starters

- *"Who do you listen to the most right now—online or in real life?"*

- *"What makes someone's opinion matter to you?"*

- *"Have you ever realized someone wasn't a good influence after the fact?"*

- *"What advice would you take seriously from someone older?"*

- *"How do you know if someone actually has your best interest in mind?"*

"

Shame, trauma, bullying, comparison, or even just not feeling seen can lead them to accept less than they deserve.

"

#sayitfirst

Chapter 7:
Building Self-Worth as a First Defense

Destiny had always been the quiet one. She got decent grades, stayed out of trouble, and didn't cause waves at home. But what most people didn't see was how often she questioned her worth.

At home, criticism came easier than praise. Her body, her clothes, her grades—it always felt like something wasn't good enough. So, when she met Zay, and he said she was beautiful and perfect just the way she was, it felt like the sun had come out.

Zay messaged her every morning, complimented her selfies, and told her how lucky he was. Destiny soaked it in. She had never felt so seen. But slowly, the compliments turned into control. He didn't want her to wear certain clothes, didn't like her talking to other guys, and constantly questioned her loyalty. And Destiny… let him.

She thought love meant making someone feel secure—even at her own expense. It wasn't until a teacher pulled her aside one day, gently asking if everything was okay, that something cracked open. The teacher didn't accuse or pry. She just listened.

Later, Destiny joined a girls' mentorship group at school. Week by week, she heard other girls talk about boundaries, self-esteem, and relationships. She realized she wasn't alone. And slowly, she started to believe she deserved more.

Destiny didn't leave overnight. But she started making small changes. She texted less. She stopped apologizing for having friends. She started saying no. Her story isn't about one big escape—but about quiet strength and the power of building self-worth from the inside out.

HELPING YOUR TEEN KNOW WHO THEY ARE—SO THEY WON'T FALL FOR SOMEONE WHO TELLS THEM WHO TO BE

When teens don't believe they matter, they're more likely to give access to people who don't deserve them.

Shame, trauma, bullying, comparison, or even just not feeling seen can lead them to accept less than they deserve. That's why the strongest boundary often starts from within— it's called self-worth.

If your teen knows their value, they'll recognize when someone's trying to discount it.

The Problem: Low Self-Worth Leads to Risky Choices

When a teen's identity isn't rooted in value, they're more likely to:

- Stay in toxic or abusive relationships out of fear of being alone

- Believe they "owe" someone access to their body or time

- Confuse attention with love, especially from older or manipulative people

- Engage in risky behaviors just to be liked, noticed, or feel something

Even high-achieving teens may silently struggle with self-worth—and hide it behind perfectionism, people-pleasing, or comparison.

What Builds Self-Worth

Self-worth doesn't come from praise alone. It grows through:

- **Belonging:** Feeling accepted as they are, not who they pretend to be

- **Voice:** Feeling like what they say matters—even when they disagree

- **Boundaries:** Knowing they can say no and still be safe and loved

- **Resilience:** Learning that failure or rejection doesn't define them

And most importantly—it's built **when safe adults model this themselves.**

Trauma and Shame: Invisible Vulnerabilities

Teens who've experienced trauma, rejection, or abuse may carry invisible weight:

- "I'm too broken to be loved."

- "If I say no, I'll be left again."

- "I deserve what happens to me."

These beliefs create openings for abusers to walk right in. That's why we must teach our kids the truth before someone else feeds them a lie.

Internal Boundaries: The Kind That Protect Without Walls

Help your teen develop boundaries from within—not just rules from the outside.

That sounds like:

- "I don't have to share my body to prove love."

- "My no is valid even if someone doesn't like it."

- "If they cross my boundary once, I'll speak up. If they do it again, I'll walk away."

- "Someone's desire doesn't override my comfort."

When they own these beliefs, they become less reactive and more grounded—even in pressure-filled moments.

Conversation Starters for Parents

- *"What do you love most about yourself that isn't physical or based on achievement?"*

- *"Do you ever feel like you have to hide parts of who you are to fit in?"*

- *"What does confidence look like to you— not the loud kind, but real self-trust?"*

- *"What's the best way to act confident even when you're nervous?"*

- *"Has anyone ever made you feel like you weren't enough? How did you respond?"*

- *"What's something you're proud of yourself for—quietly?"*

Final Thought:
Remind Them Who They Are

The world is loud with opinions, filters, and expectations.

But the strongest defense against manipulation isn't just awareness—it's identity. Teens with grounded self-worth don't need to beg for love, attention, or value. They carry it with them. And when something feels off—they walk away.

Help your child anchor that belief now, and you're protecting them long after they leave your home.

Parent Power Points: Building Self-Worth as a First Defense

Signs of Low Self-Worth

- Staying in unhealthy relationships out of fear of being alone

- Over-apologizing or avoiding conflict at all costs

- Confusing attention or flattery with real love

- Having trouble setting or maintaining boundaries

- Tolerating disrespect or manipulation in exchange for validation

What Builds Healthy Self-Worth

- Feeling seen and accepted as they are

- Knowing their voice matters—even in disagreement

- Practicing and receiving respect for boundaries

- Understanding that failure or rejection doesn't define their worth

- Having adults model confidence, repair, and healthy self-talk

Healthy Internal Boundary Beliefs

- "I don't have to share my body to prove love."

- "My no is valid—even if it disappoints someone."

- "I deserve respect without having to earn it."

- "Being wanted doesn't mean I'm safe."

- "Walking away from someone who crosses my boundary is strength—not failure."

Conversation Starters

- *"What do you like most about yourself that has nothing to do with appearance or grades?"*

- *"Do you feel safe saying no in most of your friendships?"*

- *"Has anyone ever made you feel like you had to change who you are?"*

- *"What does real confidence look like—not fake or loud, but honest?"*

- *"What helps you feel proud of yourself lately?"*

If you confront your
teen with intensity,
they'll likely shut
down—or lie.

#sayitfirst

Chapter 8:
When You Suspect Something's Off

Personal Note: The following story is drawn from my own experience as a mom. While other stories in this book are composites or anonymized to protect privacy, this one is personal. I want to share it because I know many parents may recognize themselves in my journey of trying to keep the lines of communication open with a teenager*

I started to notice something was off in my daughter's relationship. She still shared things with me—but I could tell she wasn't telling me everything. I'd bring up concerns gently, pointing out red flags I noticed. She'd listen, sometimes even agree, but it was clear she was trying really hard to make the relationship work.

This was right after her father and I divorced—a major shift in her world. She wore a happy face for me and her friends, but I knew she was carrying more than she let on.

HOW TO ASK, RESPOND, AND SUPPORT WHEN YOUR GUT TELLS YOU SOMETHING ISN'T RIGHT

You know your child better than anyone. And sometimes, you just... **feel** something shift.

Maybe it's in their eyes. Their silence. The way they don't laugh like they used to.

They say everything's "fine," but your intuition won't let it go. This chapter is for those moments—the ones where something feels off, but you're not sure what.

Subtle Signs That Deserve Attention

Teens rarely come right out and say, *"I'm being manipulated,"* or *"I'm in a toxic relationship."* But their behavior might speak for them:

- Pulling away from close friends or family

- A sudden drop in self-esteem or confidence

- Secretive behavior with their phone or online life

- Mood swings, irritability, or shutting down emotionally

- Excessive guilt, fear, or hyper-vigilance about making someone upset

- Rapid relationship changes—especially if they're overly intense

These may not confirm something dangerous is happening—but they're clues. And they deserve your attention.

How to Ask Without Accusing

If you confront your teen with intensity, they'll likely shut down—or lie.

But if you approach with curiosity and calm, they're more likely to open up.

Try:

- "I've noticed you haven't been yourself lately. Want to talk about it?"
- "You don't have to tell me everything, but I'm here for whatever you want to say."
- "You seem distracted lately—has something been bothering you?"
- "I'm not mad. I just care, and I'm paying attention."

Use "I" language over "you" accusations:

- ✓ "I'm worried" instead of ✗ "You've been acting weird"
- ✓ "I've noticed" instead of ✗ "Why are you lying?"

Your tone matters as much as your words. Stay soft—even if what you hear makes you scared.

If They Disclose Something Serious

If your teen shares that they're being pressured, manipulated, exploited, or abused:

1. **Stay calm.** Your reaction sets the tone.
2. **Believe them.** Even if it sounds confusing or unreal.
3. **Affirm their courage.** "Thank you for telling me. That was brave."
4. **Don't over-question.** Let them speak at their own pace.
5. **Ensure immediate safety.** If danger is ongoing, seek help.
6. **Involve professionals when needed.** School counselors, therapists, or advocacy centers can help.

Above all, remind them: "You're not in trouble. You're not alone. We'll get through this together."

What If They Don't Open Up Right Away?

That's okay. You're planting seeds. Every gentle check-in builds safety.

Say:

- "You don't have to talk now, but I'm here when you're ready."

- "Even if it's hard or messy, I won't be mad—I want to help."

- "You deserve to feel safe in any relationship. Always."

Conversation Starters for Parents

- *"I've noticed you've been quieter lately—how are you, really?"*

- *"Is there anyone in your life who's made you feel uncomfortable lately?"*

- *"Have you ever felt pressure to keep something secret—even if it didn't feel right?"*

- *"If something felt off in a friendship or relationship, would you feel safe telling me?"*

- *"What would help you feel supported right now—even if you're not ready to talk?"*

Final Thought:
Don't Panic. Stay Present.

Your teen doesn't need a perfect parent—they need a **safe one**.

If something's off, trust your gut—and lead with grace. The way you respond in those first moments **can shape their healing or deepen their silence.**

You're not just asking questions. You're offering a lifeline.

Parent Power Points: When You Suspect Something's Off

Subtle Warning Signs

- Sudden change in mood, withdrawal, or secrecy

- Hiding or being overly protective of their phone

- Loss of interest in previously loved activities

- Overreacting to small questions or gentle check-ins

- Intense attachment to a new friend or partner, especially if secretive

How to Ask Without Accusing

- "I've noticed you've seemed different lately. Is something on your mind?"

- "You don't have to tell me everything—but I want you to know you can."

- "I care about you. Even if it's hard, I want to understand what's going on."

- "I'm not here to judge—just to help."

If They Tell You Something Serious

- Stay calm—your reaction sets the tone.

- Thank them for trusting you and affirm their courage.

- Don't press for every detail. Let them guide the pace.

- Make a safety plan if needed and involve professionals for support.

- Reassure them: "You're not in trouble. You're not alone."

Conversation Starters

- "Has anything been weighing on you lately?"

- "Is there someone who's made you uncomfortable?"

- "You can always talk to me—even if you think I'll be upset."

- "What's something you wish you could say out loud?"

Consistency builds safety. Over time, safety opens trust. And trust invites truth.

#sayitfirst

Chapter 9:
What if They Don't Want to Talk?

Even though I kept telling her, "You can talk to me about anything," I knew she was pulling back. She wasn't shutting me out completely—but she was holding things closer.

Still, I didn't panic or feel pressured. I made sure she knew I was there. I reminded her that if she ever didn't want to talk to me, she had other trusted adults she could go to. I had built that intentionally—an inner circle of safe people.

I leaned on what I had built with her for years: openness, trust, and patience.

WHEN SILENCE IS THEIR ANSWER— WHAT TO DO NEXT

You've set aside time. You've asked all the right questions. You've even rehearsed what you'd say.

And your teen says… "I don't know."
Or worse: "I'm fine. Just drop it."

Sound familiar?

When your child shuts down or avoids hard conversations, it can feel frustrating, discouraging, or even scary. But don't let silence convince you that you've failed.

Sometimes silence isn't defiance—it's protection. Sometimes avoidance means they *want* to talk, but don't know how.

This chapter is about staying in it with them—even when they shut the door.

Why Teens Avoid Tough Talks

Silence or shutting down doesn't always mean they're hiding something. It can also be:

- Fear of being judged or punished
- Not having the language to describe what they feel
- Feeling ashamed or overwhelmed
- Thinking they'll disappoint you
- Feeling like *it won't matter* or *you'll just get mad*

Your job isn't to pry it open—it's to keep the door **unlocked**.

Timing Is Everything

Sometimes the best conversations happen:

- While driving (no eye contact = less pressure)
- While doing something side-by-side (cooking, walking, folding laundry)
- After a funny moment or something seen on social media
- *Later*, when emotions have cooled off

If they don't want to talk now, don't force it. Instead, say:

- "Okay, I hear you. I'm here when you're ready."
- "No pressure—but this door stays open."

And then? **Mean it.**

Modeling Openness

Want your teen to open up? Show them how.

Try saying:

- "I've been thinking about how I handled that the other day. I didn't love how I responded."
- "When I was your age, I wish someone had helped me through stuff like this."
- "You don't have to be perfect. Neither do I."

Modeling vulnerability and honesty sends a powerful message.

When you don't push or lecture, but simply stay present, it lowers defenses and makes room for real feelings to surface.

Re-Entering the Conversation Later

If they shut it down before, here's how to circle back without pressure:

- "I've been thinking about what you said the other day. Still open to talking more when you feel like it?"
- "Something came up that reminded me of what you were going through. Just wanted to check in."
- "I didn't forget. I'm still here."

Consistency builds safety. Over time, safety opens trust. And trust invites truth.

Conversation Starters for Parents

- *"If you ever feel like something's too hard to talk about, what's the best way I can support you?"*

- *"What helps you feel safe opening up?"*

- *"Have I ever reacted in a way that made you not want to talk to me? I can handle honesty."*

- *"Is there anything I could do differently to make conversations easier for you?"*

- *"Would you rather text or write about things than say them out loud sometimes?"*

- *"If you were in trouble but didn't want to tell me directly, how would you get my attention?"*

- *"If you ever needed me to come get you, no questions asked, would you feel comfortable calling?"*

Final Thought:
Keep Showing Up

Silence doesn't mean your teen doesn't want you. It means they want to feel safe first.

Your consistent, calm, nonjudgmental presence **is doing more than you realize**—even if they don't say it.

Keep the door unlocked.
Keep the light on.
Keep showing up.

Parent Power Points: What if They Don't Want to Talk?

Why Teens May Shut Down

- Fear of being judged, punished, or misunderstood
- Not knowing how to explain what they're feeling
- Shame, confusion, or emotional overload
- Thinking you'll be mad or disappointed
- Believing it won't make a difference

What to Say Instead of Pushing

- "Okay, I hear you. I'm here when you're ready."
- "No pressure—but my door stays open."
- "You don't have to talk now. I'll still be here later."
- "Would it help to write it instead of saying it out loud?"

How to Model Openness

- Share when you've made mistakes or felt unsure

- Admit when your reactions haven't been helpful

- Talk about hard moments you experienced at their age

- Normalize asking for help and being vulnerable

Conversation Starters

- *"What helps you feel safe opening up?"*

- *"Have I ever reacted in a way that made you want to shut down?"*

- *"Would texting or writing feel easier than talking face to face?"*

- *"Is there anything I could do differently to make things easier to talk about?"*

- *"If something ever felt too big to handle alone, how would you want me to help?"*

Chapter 10:
Keep the Door Open

When everything finally came to a head—when she hit rock bottom—she didn't come to me first. She went to her great group of trusted friends. And they came to me.

Because the door had always been open, they felt safe enough to help her reach out. And when she did come to me, she wasn't met with judgment or shame—just love, support, and a plan.

We had conversations, cried together, rebuilt, and walked through the healing. I wasn't perfect, but the groundwork had been laid. And because of that, when she needed help most, she reached for it—through the network we'd built together. Because one talk won't cut it—and that's a good thing.

If you've made it this far, you care deeply.
You're showing up. You're doing the work.
And you've likely realized something important:

This isn't a checklist. It's a relationship.

Talking to your teen about safety, consent, boundaries, identity, and relationships isn't a one-time "big talk." It's a thousand small moments. Some will be awkward. Some will be ignored. Some will land months later.

Every moment is a seed. Every moment says, *"I'm here, and I care."*

Why the Door Matters

Your teen is going to face hard things. They'll make mistakes.

They'll feel afraid, confused, embarrassed, or overwhelmed.

And when that happens, they'll ask:
 "Can I go to my parents—or will I be punished, lectured, or ignored?"

The open door is your answer.

Keeping the door open means:

- You make space for *any* conversation—even the ones that scare you
- You listen before correcting
- You allow imperfection, emotion, and messiness
- You build connection, not just compliance

Protect Without Smothering

Your job isn't to control every outcome—it's to equip and walk with them.

Teens still need boundaries. But they also need:

- Space to think for themselves
- Room to mess up without being destroyed
- Encouragement when they show honesty or self-awareness
- Connection that doesn't depend on performance

Smothering creates secrets.
Trust creates access.

Be a Safe Place, Not Just a Rule-Maker

Rules tell kids what *not* to do.
Relationship shows them *why*—and gives them someone to return to when they've done it anyway.

You can be:

- Honest without being harsh

- Curious without being invasive

- Protective without being overbearing

- Clear without being cold

Teens don't need a perfect parent. They need a consistent, safe one.

Conversation Starters for Parents

- *"What kind of adult do you hope to be one day?"*

- *"When you think about our relationship, what's one thing I do well—and one thing I could do better?"*

- *"What makes someone feel like a safe person to you?"*

- *"What do you wish more adults understood about teens?"*

- *"Is there anything you've been carrying alone that you'd want help holding?"*

- *"What's the best way for us to have serious talks without it feeling like a lecture?"*

- *"Have you ever wanted to tell me something but weren't sure how to bring it up?"*

- *"What's one thing I could do to make it easier for you to talk to me about anything?"*

- *"What's a topic you think parents should talk about more with their kids?"*

- *"What's a rule or expectation in our family that you think is fair? What's one you'd change if you could?"*

- *"If you ever needed me to listen without giving advice or asking a ton of questions, how would you let me know?"*

Final Thought:
Let This Be the Beginning

This book wasn't meant to give you perfect scripts. It was meant to start real conversations.

You might not say all the right things. That's okay.
You might get uncomfortable. That's okay too.
You might need to apologize and try again. That's actually *amazing*—because it shows your teen they can do the same.

Keep the door open. Keep coming back.
Let your child know, every step of the way:
"Whatever happens—you're not alone."

Parent Power Points: Keep the Door Open

What It Means to Keep the Door Open

- Allowing tough conversations without fear or shame

- Listening first, correcting later (or not at all)

- Letting your teen express emotions, even when it's uncomfortable

- Being available without hovering or demanding

- Following up, even when they shut down at first

Protect Without Smothering

- Provide clear expectations, but also space to grow

- Support honesty—even when it's messy or hard to hear

- Respond with curiosity instead of fear-based control

- Encourage decision-making instead of dictating

- Let them fail safely and walk with them through recovery

Conversation Starters

- *"What kind of adult do you hope to become?"*

- *"What do you wish I understood more about your world?"*

- *"Is there anything I do that makes it harder to talk to me?"*

- *"What do you need from me to feel safe being real?"*

- *"What's one thing I do that helps you feel supported?"*

Appendix:
Ways to Reach Your Teen

A Simple Way to Reach Your Teen — Even When Talking Is Tough

Sometimes the things we *want* to say to our teens don't come out the way we mean them to — or they come out at the wrong time, or in the wrong tone, or in a moment when they're not ready to hear them.

This letter is a chance to say it differently.

It's a way to put love, safety, and reassurance into words they can come back to — even on the days when they're pulling away, shutting down, or trying to figure life out on their own.

You don't have to write it perfectly.
You just have to write it honestly.

Use the template as-is, or change every line.
Make it funny, emotional, short, long — whatever fits your relationship.
What matters most is this: **your teen hears from you in a way they can keep.**

A spoken conversation can get lost in a moment.
A written one becomes something they can return to when they need it most.

Letter To Your Teen

Dear __________________,

I know growing up in today's world isn't easy. There's pressure—from friends, from social media, from everywhere—to look, act, and feel a certain way. I don't always have the right words, but I want you to know this: my love for you is constant, and my door is always open.

You can come to me about anything. Even if it's uncomfortable. Even if you think I'll be upset. Even if you've made a mistake. Nothing you could say will make me stop caring or listening.

I want you to always know that your voice matters. Your "no" matters. Your feelings matter. You deserve to be treated with respect, kindness, and honesty—both online and in person.

My hope for you is that you'll trust yourself, set boundaries that protect your peace, and remember that your worth isn't defined by anyone else's opinion.

I am here to guide you, cheer for you, and help you navigate whatever life brings. You don't have to have it all figured out—you just have to keep talking.

With all my love,

____

(Your Name)

Reflection Prompts for Parents

- What do I want my teen to always remember about our relationship?

- What boundaries or values do I want to affirm in this letter?

- What do I want them to know if they ever feel scared or ashamed?

- How can I express both love and safety in my own words?

- What reassurance do I want to give if they make a mistake or face something hard?

Continue the Conversation

Cerise Woodard is available for training, seminars, workshops, and keynote presentations for parents, educators, healthcare professionals, faith communities, and organizations committed to prevention, awareness, and empowerment.

Through trauma-informed, practical, and engaging education, Cerise equips adults and communities with tools to recognize risk, reduce vulnerability, and create safer environments for youth and families.

To inquire about booking Cerise for your next event or training, connect below:

Cerise Woodard, RN SANE-A | Founder, BoundlessHer
She Was Bound. Now She's Boundless.
Awareness. Advocacy. Awakening.

Email: boundlessher@gmail.com

Website: www.boundlessher.com

Instagram: @boundlessherofficial

Facebook: BoundlessHer Official

About the Author

Cerise Woodard is a passionate advocate, educator, and forensic nurse with over 30 years of nursing experience. Her love for her daughter and her role as a proud bonus mom and grandmother have shaped her mission: helping families protect what matters most and closing the gaps that leave youth vulnerable.

Cerise became deeply attuned to the growing crisis of missing and exploited children after seeing real-time alerts on social media. As a parent, her heart broke. She couldn't ignore the pain of mothers across the country searching for their children. That empathy quickly turned into a fire to understand—and disrupt—the system behind the disappearances.

Her research exposed a thriving trafficking industry that feeds on the vulnerability of youth. Since then, Cerise has dedicated herself to raising awareness, training communities, and educating families about how to spot the signs and close the gaps that predators exploit. She believes one of the most powerful ways to disrupt the cycle is by cutting off the supply—and that starts with equipping our kids before someone else does.

This guide is her invitation to parents everywhere: don't wait for something to happen. Start the conversation now.